GREEN LANTERN CORPS

VOLUME 1 FEARSOME

GREEN LANTERN CORPS

VOLUME 1 FEARSOME

PETER J. **TOMASI** writer

FERNANDO **PASARIN** penciller

GERALDO **BORGES**   CLAUDE **ST. AUBIN** additional pencillers

SCOTT **HANNA** inker

GABE **ELTAEB** colorist

PAT **BROSSEAU**   DAVE **SHARPE** letterers

DOUG **MAHNKE**, CHRISTIAN **ALAMY** & RANDY **MAYOR**
collection cover artists

BRIAN CUNNINGHAM Editor – Original Series DARREN SHAN Assistant Editor – Original Series
PETER HAMBOUSSI Editor ROBBIN BROSTERMAN Design Director – Books
ROBBIE BIEDERMAN Publication Design

BOB HARRAS Senior VP – Editor-in-Chief, DC Comics

DIANE NELSON President DAN DIDIO and JIM LEE Co-Publishers
GEOFF JOHNS Chief Creative Officer
JOHN ROOD Executive VP – Sales, Marketing & Business Development
AMY GENKINS Senior VP – Business & Legal Affairs NAIRI GARDINER Senior VP – Finance
JEFF BOISON VP – Publishing Planning MARK CHIARELLO VP – Art Direction & Design
JOHN CUNNINGHAM VP – Marketing TERRI CUNNINGHAM VP – Editorial Administration
ALISON GILL Senior VP – Manufacturing & Operations HANK KANALZ Senior VP – Vertigo & Integrated Publishing
JAY KOGAN VP – Business & Legal Affairs, Publishing JACK MAHAN VP – Business Affairs, Talent
NICK NAPOLITANO VP – Manufacturing Administration SUE POHJA VP – Book Sales
COURTNEY SIMMONS Senior VP – Publicity BOB WAYNE Senior VP – Sales

GREEN LANTERN CORPS VOLUME 1: FEARSOME

DC Comics, 1700 Broadway, New York, NY 10019
A Warner Bros. Entertainment Company
Printed by RR Donnelley, Salem, VA, USA. 5/31/13. First Printing.
ISBN: 978-1-4012-3702-8.

SUSTAINABLE FORESTRY INITIATIVE

Certified Chain of Custody
At Least 20% Certified Forest Content
www.sfiprogram.org
SFI-01042
APPLIES TO TEXT STOCK ONLY

Library of Congress Cataloging-in-Publication Data

Tomasi, Peter.
Green Lantern Corps. Volume 1, Fearsome / Peter J. Tomasi.
p. cm.
ISBN 978-1-4012-3701-1
1. Graphic novels. I. Pasarin, Fernando. II. Hanna, Scott. III.
Title. IV. Title: Fearsome.
PN6728.G742T6 2012
741.5'973—dc23
2012018769

TRIUMPH OF THE WILL

PETER J. TOMASI writer FERNANDO PASARIN penciller SCOTT HANNA inker cover by DOUG MAHNKE & CHRISTIAN ALAMY with RANDY MAYOF

THE SOFTWARE PROGRAM IN THAT RING IS SIMPLY AMAZING.

SAY THE WORD, AND I'LL PUT YOU AND BILL GATES TOGETHER AND STRUCTURE A DEAL THAT WOULD MAKE YOU A RICH--

THERE'S NO PROGRAM. THE RING READS MY THOUGHTS. WHAT I SEE IN MY HEAD IS WHAT I CAN *MAKE* OUT HERE.

IT'S GOT WEIGHT AND EDGES.

HARD LIGHT, SOFT LIGHT, ONE OUNCE, ONE TON, ALL I NEED TO DO IS THINK IT AND THE RING INSTANTLY PROJECTS IT.

YES, THE *PUBLICITY* FACTOR OF HAVING A GREEN LANTERN FOR AN ARCHITECT IS ALL WELL AND GOOD...

...BUT THESE *SAFETY* MEASURES ARE INCREDIBLY COST *PROHIBITIVE,* MISTER STEWART. YOU'RE ASKING US TO GO ABOVE *AND* BEYOND WHAT EVERY OTHER BUILDING OWNER IS DOING IN THE CITY.

BECAUSE IT'S THE *RIGHT* THING TO DO, AND *I'M* NOT TAKING SHORTCUTS.

C'MON, AS LONG AS WE'RE UP TO *CODE* WHY DO YOU INSIST ON--

IT'S ABOUT HAVING A *CODE OF HONOR,* NOT A CODE OF WEALTH.

WE'RE ALL FAMILIAR *AND* APPRECIATIVE OF YOUR *MARINE CORPS* SERVICE, MISTER STEWART, BUT IT DOESN'T MEAN WE HAVE TO HAVE YOUR *MOTTOS* THROWN OUR WAY.

MOTHERS, FATHERS, SONS, AND DAUGHTERS SPEND A BIG PART OF THEIR LIVES INSIDE THE STEEL AND GLASS WE BUILD AROUND THEM TO BRING HOME A PAYCHECK. THE LEAST WE CAN DO IS MAKE SURE THEY'RE SAFE DOING IT.

AND THESE *S.P.I.R.* NOTATIONS--EXPLAIN TO ME HOW I CONVINCE MY BOARD TO APPROVE SUCH A PRODIGIOUS OUTLAY OF FUNDS FOR SOMETHING WE'RE NOT EVEN *LEGALLY* OBLIGATED TO DO, HMM?

SURE, LET ME TAKE A CRACK AT IT.

AIIEEE

YAGGH

TELL YOUR BOARD THE NEXT TIME THE JUSTICE LEAGUE OR THE TEEN TITANS HAVE A MAJOR THROWDOWN WITH SOME *MAJOR NASTIES* OR A 9.2 EARTHQUAKE ROCKS THE CITY, THE SPECIALLY DEVELOPED SUPER-POWERED INCLUSION REINFORCEMENT THEY VOTED FOR WILL MAINTAIN THE STRUCTURAL INTEGRITY OF THEIR BUILDING AND KEEP IT FROM FALLING DOWN AND KILLING THOUSANDS OF PEOPLE.

OR BETTER YET, TELL THEM IT'LL KEEP THEIR LIABILITY AND COURT COSTS DOWN. I'M SURE *THAT'S* SOMETHING THEY CAN WRAP THEIR HEADS AROUND.

YOU *ASSURED* US YOU'D KEEP THE BUDGET UNDER CONTROL.

NOT AT THE RISK OF HUMAN LIFE I DIDN'T.

THE CITY ENGINEERS AND THE MAYOR'S OFFICE *APPROVED* ALL THE CODE SPECS WITHOUT YOUR UPGRADED AND UNNECESSARY SAFETY MEASURES.

SIRAM AND BBOC. WE WERE RECRUITS TOGETHER.

I'M SENDING THEM BACK TO OA FOR INTERMENT *RIGHT NOW.*

WE GOT A CHANCE TO BURY OUR OWN TODAY, BUT HOW DO WE BURY A WORLD?

YOU DON'T.

YOU CAN'T.

WE SHOULD LEAVE THIS HORRIFIC SITE AS A *REMINDER* OF WHAT HAPPENED HERE SO *WHEN* WE BRING THE BASTARDS TO JUSTICE WE'LL *MAKE THEM* DO THE BURYING.

I *LIKE* THE WAY YOU THINK, SHERIFF.

HOW ABOUT WE *FIND* THEM FIRST BEFORE WE START DREAMING UP WAYS TO--

TRANS-LUMINAL DISPLACEMENT DETECTED IN SECTOR 3599. ENERGY SIGNATURE IDENTICAL TO LATEST VARIANCE.

FINDING'S DONE, JOHNNY!

NOW LET'S GO KICK THEIR ASS!

SPLASSH

I HAVE MISSED
THE SOUND OF
THE SEA.

AS HAVE
ALL OUR PEOPLE,
YOUR WORSHIP.

WHAT
IS IT?

THERE'S
A PROBLEM
ON XABAS.

THEN
ADDRESS
IT.

NOW.

CHOPPING FINGERS OFF GREEN LANTERNS AND STAKING THEM TO THE--

RRRGH, I COULD CRUSH YOUR HEADS AND NOT LOSE ANY SLEEP OVER IT!

FIRST THE WATER FROM NERRO AND NOW THE TREES ON XABAS--

TREES? IT'S NOT TREES WE WANT.

THE CITIZENS OF THIS PLANET ARE INCREDIBLY UNIQUE AND VALUABLE. THEY EXHALE A SPECIFIC TYPE OF CHEMICAL THAT ACTUALLY FORMS A LIVABLE ATMOSPHERE.

AT LEAST WE STOPPED YOU BEFORE YOU COULD RAVAGE OTHER PLANETS.

STOP US? THIS WAS THE LAST STAGE OF OUR MISSION.

WE'VE TAKEN ALL THAT WE NEED.

WHY THE SEVERED FINGERS? WHAT HAS THE CORPS DONE TO YOU?

WHAT HASN'T IT DONE?

ALL RIGHT, ENOUGH YAPPING. WE'RE DRAGGING YOU BACK TO OA.

WE'RE NOT GOING ANYWHERE, AND NEITHER ARE YOU.

SALAAK! WE NEED REINFORCEMENTS AT OUR POSITION ON XABAS NOW!

WHAT IS THE STATUS OF--

I GOT NO DAMN TIME TO EXPLAIN THE STATUS!

WE NEED AS MANY RING SLINGERS YOU GOT OR WE'RE TOAST AND SO ARE THE PEOPLE OF THIS PLANET!

WHAT ARE YOU UP AGAINST, GARDNER?

WE'RE UP AGAINST UNFRIENDLIES WHO ARE ALMOST IMMUNE TO OUR FREAKIN' RINGS!

THAT'S IMPOSSIBLE.

YEAH-- WELL TELL THAT TO THEM!

I DON'T KNOW HOW MUCH LONGER WE CAN HOLD THE-- KZZKK

TRANSMISSION ENDED.

IF GARDNER'S REQUESTING ASSISTANCE, THE SITUATION IS DIRE.

ALL UNASSIGNED LANTERNS REPORT TO QUADRANT 4 FOR IMMEDIATE MISSION COMMAND!

THIS IS NOT A DRILL! REPEAT, THIS IS NOT A DRILL!

LANTERNS! PROCEED WITHOUT DELAY TO THE PLANET XABAS.

I HAVE UPLOADED YOUR RINGS WITH LIVE STREAMING FROM THE COMBAT ZONE TO KEEP YOU INFORMED OF CURRENT CONFLICT STATUS DURING YOUR THREE-HOUR TREK TO THE--

YOU CAN DIVERT ONLY SO MUCH POWER TO KEEP US IN CHECK AND STILL MAINTAIN YOUR SHIELD INTEGRITY.

YOU WILL ALL DIE SOON.

THEN YOU'RE NOT GOING TO MIND IF WE PICK YOUR BRAIN TO HELP US EXPLOIT ANY WEAK SPOTS IN YOUR LITTLE ARMY--

--SO AT LEAST THE LAST THING WE DO HERE IS LET THE CORPS BACK ON OA LEARN EVERYTHING THEY CAN ON HOW TO *BEAT* YOUR ASS!

I DON'T THINK SO...

RING! WHAT'S HAPPENING TO THEM?

THEY ARE SHUTTING THEMSELVES DOWN.

DEFINE "SHUTTING DOWN."

THEY ARE WILLING THEMSELVES TO DIE.

BODY SCAN COMPLETE.

SPECIES UNRECOGNIZED. NOT ON FILE.

UNRECOGNIZED? WHAT ELSE?

THESE BEINGS POSSESS AN INNATE RESERVE OF WILLPOWER THAT IS OVERWHELMING AND NOT IN PROPORTION TO THEIR RELATIVELY COMMON FORMS.

DID YOU HEAR THAT? THAT'S WHY THEY'VE BEEN ABLE TO TAKE OUR BLASTS.

THAT CONFIRMS IT, GUY--WE'RE FIGHTING WILLPOWER WITH WILLPOWER!

WELL, THAT TIDBIT'S NOT GONNA DO US ANY GOOD RIGHT NOW--

--'CAUSE I THINK IT'S DO OR DIE TIME, JOHNNY--

DO OR--

SALAAK, YOU BEAUTIFUL UGLY BASTARD --

PAASH

RING, TRANSLATE: EVERYONE STAY CALM AND REMAIN CLOSE.

ᑎᑎᑌᒎᔕᒎᐃᑎᒋ ᐢᒎᐃᔕ ᑕᐃᔕᖿ ᐃᐢᔕ ᑌᑎᔭᐃᑎ ᑕᔕᐃᑎᖿ.

DON'T KNOW HOW YOU PULLED ALL THOSE GL'S HERE WITHOUT BLOWING A GASKET, BUT I HOPE YOU BOOKED A *RETURN TICKET* FOR ALL OF US.

SURE DID... BUT WE DON'T HAVE MUCH TIME, WHOEVER THEY ARE...THEY'RE MASSING AGAIN FOR ANOTHER ATTACK.

THE LANTERNS THAT CAME WITH ME WILL FORM A DEFENSE RING...

...SO WE CAN GET YOU AND THESE REMAINING PEOPLE OUT OF HERE...

YOUR EYES ARE *BLEEDING*--OR MAYBE WE CAN BUY YOU SOME RECOVERY TIME BEFORE YOU TRY TELEPORTING AGAIN.

I'M FINE... JUST NEED TO FOCUS...

HERE COMES THE SECOND WAVE!

THEY'RE PENETRATING OUR FIELD OF FIRE--

--AND THE DEFENSE RING!

CONTINUE THE BARRAGE!

THEY'RE CLOSING IN FAST!

I DON'T CARE IF WE DIE TODAY--BUT I'M NOT JUST GOING TO STAND HERE!

LET'S GO HIT SOMEBODY!

I'M WITH HANNU! LET'S BLAST AS MANY--

STAY STILL, DAMN IT!

...EVERYONE...
EVERYONE
BACK...?

UM,
YEAH...

SOMETHING'S
WRONG...LIKE I
LEFT SOME OF THEM
BEHIND...PLEASE...
TELL ME THE TRUTH...
IS EVERYONE
ALL RIGHT...?

YOU SAVED OUR
BACON, KID--GOT US
ALL BACK SAFE AND
SOUND TO OA.

YOU DID
IT. REST EASY
NOW...

..OH...OKAY...
GOOD...FOR A
SECOND THERE I
THOUGHT I
SCREWED--

GET THIS
SLIMEBALL TO
SALAAK.

I'M GONNA PEEL
HIS BRAIN BACK UNTIL WE KNOW
WHAT HE ATE FOR BREAKFAST WHEN
HE WAS THREE--WE'RE GONNA SEE
WHAT MAKES YOU *TICK*, LAB RAT--

--BECAUSE
FOREWARNED IS
FOREARMED.

WE MAY HAVE LOST TODAY,
BUT WE'RE DAMN WELL
WINNING *TOMORROW*...

WHAT ARE YOU WAITING FOR?!? COME ON!

WE'RE NOT GOING DOWN WITHOUT A FIGHT!

IT'S A FIGHT YOU'VE ALREADY LOST, LANTERNS.

FIRE THESE FEEBLE BLASTS AT US ALL YOU WANT.

YOU'VE EXHAUSTED YOUR ENERGY SUPPLY.

THE BEST WEAPONS ARE THE ONES THAT *CAN'T* BE USED AGAINST YOURSELF--

--BUT ON *OTHERS!*

NO!

WE'RE UNARMED--WE'VE GOT NO OTHER DEVICE THAT CAN INFLICT HARM ON YOU.

EXCEPT A *MIND*, WHICH CAN *ALWAYS* BE USED AS A WEAPON.

UNDER THE *STAR TREATY OF AV-ENEG* YOU'RE *REQUIRED* TO ACCEPT OUR SURRENDER AND TREAT US AS--

WE SPIT ON ALL *TREATIES*, AND SURRENDER'S *ABHORRENT* TO YOU AS IT IS TO US. I CAN SEE IT IN YOUR EYES.

THAT'S WHY I FEEL YOU STILL NEED...

WE'VE BEEN PUMPING YA WITH A SELECT SEDATIVE-- TAKING THE EDGE OFF YOUR WILLPOWER SO YOU COULD BE A BIT MORE...PLIABLE.

AND HOW IS *THAT* WORKING FOR YOU, *GUY GARDNER?*

NOT GOOD, ACTUALLY. YOU'RE A TOUGH NUT, BUT THANKS FOR ASKING.

TOOK ME HOURS JUST TO GET ALL YOUR ARMOR OFF. BUT AS YOU CAN SEE, I FINALLY REMOVED YOUR HEADGEAR.

WITH A FACE LIKE YOURS, I SEE WHY YA WENT WITH A MASK.

AT LEAST NOW YOU'RE READY--

--FOR YOUR CLOSE-UP!

OOPS, MY BAD--A LITTLE *TOO* CLOSE, HUH?

SKRAK

--MAYBE DEAD'S THE WAY TO GO HERE!

KRAK

TWO PROBLEMS: ONE, LANTERN SAAREK OF SECTOR 773 WAS *KILLED* ON RYUT. TWO, THERE WILL BE *NO* EXECUTION OF A PRISONER WHILE I AM--

IT'S *INTIMIDATION* FER CRISSAKES--IT'S CALLED "GOOD COP, BAD COP," SALAAK--OR IN YOUR CASE SIMPLY "*IDIOT COP*"!

YOU REALIZE IT'S ONLY A MATTER OF TIME BEFORE WE FIND OUT *WHO* YOU PEOPLE ARE, HOW YOU'RE OPERATING THAT *PORTAL TECH,* AND *WHY* YOU'RE *SLAUGHTERING ENTIRE PLANETS* ACROSS THE UNIVERSE, RIGHT?

YOU'VE HAD NO LUCK IDENTIFYING ME IN YOUR DATABASE, BUT FEEL FREE TO KEEP TRYING.

OH, WE'RE GONNA DO MORE THAN *TRY,* CHUCKLES.

BONK

UGNN

WE'RE GONNA DIG.

DEEP.

Isamot Kol

--NO--
STOP--

--GET BACK--
DON'T COME
ANY--

STAY
AWAY FROM
ME!

...GET
HOLD OF
YOURSELF,
DAMN IT...
JUST A BAD
DREAM...

...NO
FEAR,
MAN...

NO
FEAR.

"...I THOUGHT WE WERE ALL GONNA DIE."

WHAT THE HELL--

BE PREPARED TO LOSE YOUR WILL AND MAYBE YOUR LIVES...

THAT'S IMPOSSIBLE.

--IT WAS LIKE REACHING INTO A DARK CLOSET THAT FOLLOWED YOU EVERYWHERE AND BEING ABLE TO RELOAD THE RING WHEN YOUR POWER WAS SHOT TO HELL.

WE WERE ALWAYS THE KEEPERS OF OUR OWN BATTERIES.

NNN...

WHUMP

THAT WAS NOT THE CASE.

THE BATTERIES YOU SO CONVENIENTLY PULLED OUT OF NOWHERE ACTUALLY CAME FROM SOMEWHERE, AND IT SEEMS THESE... BEINGS WERE RESPONSIBLE FOR TENDING TO THEM.

ALL THE GUARDIANS TOLD US A LITTLE WHILE BACK WAS THAT THE WORMHOLE SITUATION BECAME UNTENABLE-- THAT FROM HERE ON OUT WE WOULD BE RESPONSIBLE FOR OUR OWN BATTERIES' LOCATIONS.

THEY NEVER MENTIONED THE BATTERIES HAD A POINT OF ORIGIN--AN ACTUAL PLACE THAT WE WERE PULLING THEM FROM...

I STILL DON'T UNDERSTAND. WHY NOT HELP US FIGHT THESE GUYS? THEY'RE NO WALK IN THE PARK.

STORMWATCH WILL GET INVOLVED IF IT NEEDS TO. FOR NOW, THE CORPS SERVES OUR NEEDS TO COMBAT THIS THREAT, SO DO NOT FAIL.

FOR HERE IS WHAT THESE KEEPERS WANT...

YOU'VE GOT TO BE AMONG HE WORST *POOZERS* I'VE EVER HAD THE DISPLEASURE OF TRAINING!

KILOWOG, I NEED TO--

THIS BETTER BE IMPORTANT, GUY!

I'M IN THE MIDDLE OF TEACHING RECRUITS HOW *NOT* TO DIE!

C'MON, YA BIG LUG, WALK WITH ME, TALK WITH ME.

WHAT IS IT?

I NEED A LIST.

WHAT KIND OF LIST?

TOP O' THE MORNING TO YOU, GUY.

IT'S BEEN A WHILE SINCE YOU OR LANTERN RAYNER OPENED THE BAR YOURSELF.

I BEEN KINDA BUSY AND WE'RE NOT OPEN YET, BEAUTIFUL.

WOULD YOU LIKE ME TO GO OVER THE ACCOUNTS RECEIVABLE INVOICES WITH YOU INSTEAD OF THE MANAGER?

NO PAPER PUSHING FOR ME, I'M HERE ON OTHER BUSINESS.

WELL WHADDAYA KNOW...

RING, SCAN AREA AND COMPARE IT TO STEWART'S ORIGINAL ARCHITECTURAL PLANS.

SHOW ANY STRUCTURAL DEVIATION THAT'D--

...I GOT ME SOME GROUNDHOG PROBLEMS.

WHEN KILOWOG SAID THERE WERE A FEW OF YOU LEFT, HE WASN'T KIDDING.

DON'T FRET, BOY, THERE'S MORE OF US SUCKING WIND THAN YOU REALIZE...

...THEY JUST AIN'T HERE RIGHT NOW.

WHAT BRINGS YOU DOWN TO OUR WATERING HOLE?

WELL, IT'S ACTUALLY MY HOLE, LEE, WARRIORS SITS ON TOP OF THIS.

WE NOTICED THAT, BUT DON'T WORRY, WE DON'T MIND.

YEAH, THE FREE BOOZE HAS BEEN A PLUS.

WHAT'S WITH ALL THE SMOKE, ALDO?

MY LEG CATCHES ON FIRE FROM TIME TO TIME-- LOST IT IN A BATTLE WITH THE KHUNDS WHEN I WAS A RECRUIT.

WHO'S THIS GUY?

I AM THE *MARTIAN MANHUNTER*, AND THE ARROGANCE I FEEL WITHIN YOUR MINDS ASTOUNDS ME. I PROVIDE YOU LANTERNS WITH THIS INFORMATION SOLELY BECAUSE IT FALLS OUTSIDE THE WATCH OF MY...USUAL ASSOCIATES.

GUY, CAN HE BE *TRUSTED*...?

I DON'T LIKE HIM EITHER, SHERIFF, BUT HIS INTEL SEEMS ON THE LEVEL.

SO YOU'RE A TELEPATH? WHAT I GOT UP HERE IS MINE AND MINE *ALONE*. I DON'T NEED ANY *VISITORS*.

WHEN I AM DONE, YOU WON'T HAVE ANY MEMORY OF ME OR WHAT I DO HERE.

NOT TOO HAPPY ABOUT WORKING WITH LANTERNS I DON'T KNOW-- ESPECIALLY ONES THAT LOOK LIKE THEY CAME OFF THE *SCRAP HEAP*.

I HEAR YOU DON'T LIKE TO USE YOUR POWER RING.

THAT'S RIGHT, *LEE*, I *RELY* ON MY *OWN* STRENGTH FIRST BEFORE *RESORTING* TO IT.

WHAT ARE YOU, *STUPID* OR SOME-THING?

WHERE'S THE REST OF YOU, *GIZZARD BOY?* SEEM TO BE *SHY* A FEW PARTS.

DON'T WORRY, FLINT, THEY'LL GROW BACK, BUT I CAN'T SAY THE SAME FOR YOUR HEAD ONCE I *SLICE* IT OFF.

MISSING SOME ARMS AND LEGS, BUT AT LEAST YOU GOT SOME GUTS.

I THOUGHT THIS WAS A UNIT OPERATION--THAT WE WERE GOING IN *ALONE*.

WE'RE PART OF THE UNIT, SO GET OVER IT, BRONCHUK.

THE ONLY THING I'D LIKE TO GET *OVER* ON IS YOU, BRIK.

YOU JUST WENT AND BROKE MY HEART.

WE'VE NOT ONLY GOT LANTERNS IN JEOPARDY BUT WE HAVE WHOLE *WORLDS* IN THE LINE OF FIRE HERE SO I WANT EVERY-ONE TO SHUT UP AND *CUT THE CRAP!*

WE'RE DEALIN' WITH A RACE THAT WANTS TO INVADE OA AND STEAL THE CENTRAL POWER BATTERY! THEY MADE MINCEMEAT OUT OF US BEFORE--NO REASON THEY CAN'T DO IT AGAIN RIGHT AT OUR *DOORSTEP*.

MANHUNTER, LET'S GET THIS *DONE* WITH.

WHAK

"OPEN YOUR MINDS TO ME, LANTERNS..."

"...AFTER NUMEROUS SITUATIONS OF POWER RINGS BEING DEPLETED AT CRITICAL MOMENTS, THE GUARDIANS DECIDED IT WAS IMPERATIVE THAT THEIR LANTERN CORPS HAVE SWIFT AND EFFORTLESS *ACCESS* TO THEIR INDIVIDUAL POWER BATTERY WHEN A RECHARGE WAS REQUIRED.

"THIS *NEED* LED TO A *UNIQUE WORLD* THAT EXISTED AT THE EDGE OF THE UNIVERSE CALLED *URAK*.

"THEY WOULD BE PROVIDED FOR IN PERPETUITY IF THEY WATCHED OVER THE BATTERIES LIKE A SHEPHERD OVER HIS SHEEP.

"FROM THAT POINT ON THEY WERE CALLED *THE KEEPERS,* AND ONLY THE GUARDIANS KNEW OF THEIR LOCATION AND EXISTENCE.

"DUE TO THE PLANET'S *UNUSUAL COMPOSITION* THE BATTERIES FUNCTIONED LIKE A CROP--A CROP OF ENERGY THAT FED THE PLANET AND, IN TURN, FED THE PEOPLE ON THE PLANET.

"OVER TIME IT *INFUSED* THEIR ALREADY SINGULAR DNA WITH AN INCREDIBLY POTENT *FORCE OF WILL*.

"IT WAS AN EXTRAORDINARY PLANET THAT ALLOWED THE GUARDIANS TO *ATTUNE* THE RINGS AND THE POWER BATTERIES TO THE *STRANGE AND DISTINCTIVE* ELEMENTS AT ITS CORE...

"BUT THERE WAS A PROBLEM.

"...WHICH IN TURN CREATED AN *INSTANTANEOUS* TEMPORAL CONDUIT THAT ALLOWED ANY LANTERN IN ANY SECTOR TO IMMEDIATELY *SUMMON* THEIR BATTERY TO THEIR PRESENT POSITION.

"THE INNER-SPACE OF THE PLANET MAY HAVE BEEN ADVANTAGEOUS TO THE GUARDIANS' STRATEGY, BUT ITS *INHABITANTS* WERE BARELY SUBSISTING ON THE BARREN SURFACE.

"THE GUARDIANS MADE A *PACT* WITH THESE PEOPLE.

"THEY *HELPED* THEM BUILD A WORLD.

"...UNTIL A SHORT TIME AGO, WHEN *WITHOUT* REASON OR WARNING, THE GUARDIANS *SUDDENLY REMOVED* EACH AND EVERY BATTERY FROM THE KEEPERS' CUSTODY.

"THEIR WORLD BEGAN TO DIE."

YOUR EXHAUSTION IS PALPABLE. THREE DAYS WITHOUT FOOD OR WATER-- A HARSH JOURNEY THAT I'M SURE WAS FRAUGHT WITH--

...BEATINGS AND BELLIGERENCE... NOTHING WE'RE NOT USED TO...

YES, WELL, MY WARRIORS DO NEED TO TAKE OUT THEIR AGGRESSION ON *SOMEONE*, AND IF WE CAN'T PUNISH THE GUARDIANS JUST YET, WHO BETTER THAN THE PEOPLE WHO REPRESENT THEM THROUGHOUT THE UNIVERSE.

WHAT THE HELL ARE YOU TALKING ABOUT-- WHAT DID THE GUARDIANS EVER DO--

THEY HAVE DONE QUITE ENOUGH, LANTERN!

I HAVE LED MY PEOPLE THROUGH HORRORS YOU CAN ONLY IMAGINE!

BUT, IT'S A LONG STORY AND ONE YOU WILL NOT HAVE TIME TO HEAR.

ARRHHHRRR!

DO YOU RECALL PASSING THAT LARGE PLAIN OF LANTERN SYMBOLS ETCHED IN THE GROUND?

HARD TO MISS-- YOUR *"WARRIORS"* MADE A POINT OF KICKING US ACROSS IT.

WE'VE KEPT THAT AREA *BARREN* AS A REMINDER OF WHAT WE GAINED AND WHAT WE LOST THANKS TO THE *BETRAYAL* OF YOUR BLUE-SKINNED OVERLORDS.

AND I'VE COME TO BELIEVE THAT *LOSS* SHOULD BE A *SHARED* EXPERIENCE AMONG *OLD FRIENDS.*

WE WILL NOT STOP UNTIL *EVERY* RING FINGER OF THE CORPS IS CUT OFF AND PLANTED IN THE LANTERN HOLES YOU PASSED--THEN I'M GOING TO *RIP* THE CENTRAL POWER BATTERY FROM OA AND SET IT DOWN HERE, WHERE *MY* WORLD WILL BECOME THE CENTER OF THE UNIVERSE.

BUT, WE'RE GETTING AHEAD OF OURSELVES.

THANKS TO THE STARGATE MY PEOPLE HAVE SACRIFICED THEIR VERY LIVES FOR, OUR WORLD IS STRONGER NOW THAN IT'S EVER BEEN.

WE'VE TAKEN THE FINEST RESOURCES FROM THE PLANETS WE WANTED--PRISTINE WATER, AIR, FOOD, ANIMALS--AND *REPLENISHED* THE DYING WORLD YOUR *GUARDIANS* LEFT US.

ALL THAT REMAINS IS A *RECKONING,* AND THAT CAN ONLY BE ACHIEVED ONCE YOU *COMMAND* YOUR RING TO ANSWER THE QUESTION I HAVE ASKED OVER AND OVER AGAIN.

WHAT IS THE *VIBRATIONAL MATRIX SIGNATURE* THAT WILL ALLOW US TO *BREACH* OA'S ORBITAL FORCE-FIELD WITHOUT ALERTING THEM TO OUR STARGATE?

GO TO HELL.

AARHHHHHH!

LET'S SEE WHOSE WILLPOWER WILL BREAK FIRST.

HOLD TIGHT, VANDOR--

SMAASSH

--WE'RE GETTING OUT OF HERE!

YOUR RING--THERE WAS NO POWER LEFT--HOW DID YOU GET IT TO WORK?!?

USED THE ENERGY HE WAS ZAPPING US WITH LIKE A PILOT LIGHT-- IGNITED WHATEVER *RESIDUAL POWER* WAS LEFT IN THE RING AND CHANNELED IT SOMEHOW.

YOU *WILLED* US OUT OF THERE, JOHN--YOU DID WHAT YOU HAD TO DO AND YOU PUT ONE LAST CHARGE IN THE RING!

I'M AFRAID THE CHARGE WASN'T BIG ENOUGH--WE'RE RUNNING ON FUMES, VANDOR--WE'RE NOT GETTING VERY FAR.

AT LEAST YOU GAVE US A CHANCE TO PICK OUR PLACE TO DIE, JOHN, AND MORE IMPORTANT--

--WE DON'T HAVE TO DO IT UPSIDE DOWN.

WELL, VANDOR, LIKE J.R.R. TOLKIEN SAID--OUT OF THE FRYING PAN AND INTO THE--

THE PLANET NERRO. 24 HOURS LATER.

WHY ARE WE *HERE* AND NOT BEING BROUGHT BEFORE A GUARDIAN TRIBUNAL OR PLACED IN YOUR SCIENCELLS?

WE *DEMAND* TO SEE--

YOU CAN *SHOVE* YOUR DEMAND BECAUSE YOU'VE ALREADY *HAD* YOUR TRIBUNAL--*WE* PRESENTED THE FACTS OF YOUR WAR OF AGGRESSION AND THE GUARDIANS RULED.

OF COURSE YOU DID, AND I ASSUME THE VERDICT WAS *GUILTY.*

GOOD GUESS, CHUCKLES, AND THEY ALSO LIKED MY *CREATIVE* SENTENCING IDEA.

AND WHAT *IDEA* IS THAT?

START DIGGING.

DIGGING WHAT?

GRAVES.

YOU'RE BURYING EVERY LAST ONE OF YOUR INNOCENT VICTIMS.

ROD
REIS

PETER J. TOMASI writer   CLAUDE ST. AUBIN penciller   SCOTT HANNA inker   cover by IVAN REIS, JOE PRADO & ROD REIS

AND NOW I, *LANTERN MORRO, CRYPTKEEPER OF THE CORPS,* WILL ASSIST YOU ON YOUR FINAL JOURNEY...

...A *JOURNEY* THAT ONLY THOSE WHO HAVE MADE...

...THE *GREATEST SACRIFICE* OF ALL CAN TAKE.

IT IS *OUR* PRIVILEGE TO BE IN *YOUR* PRESENCE AT THIS MOMENTOUS TIME.

AND WHAT I PERFORM NOW IS TO HONOR YOU FOR *ALL ETERNITY.*

...NO EVIL *ESCAPED* HIS SIGHT.

LET THOSE WHO WORSHIP EVIL'S MIGHT...

...BEWARE *KIRRT'S* POWER...

I'M SURE I DON'T HAVE TO TELL YOU WHICH *DISCONCERTING ACTION* MY PRESIDENT TOOK.

WITH WORLD WAR II ROLLING IN MY HEAD I DID THE MATH, AND GUESS WHAT?

YOU TRY OUR PATIENCE, GARDNER. WE ARE QUITE *FAMILIAR* WITH THE HISTORY OF YOUR HOME WORLD, AND THIS ATTITUDE OF--

TWO SINESTRO CORPS SOLDIERS, WHO'VE *HAPPILY* KILLED THOUSANDS OF PEOPLE, *WASN'T WORTH* NEARLY AS MUCH AS SAVING THOUSANDS OF INNOCENT LIVES INCLUDING THE KEEPERS' ENTIRE FREAKIN' ARMY AND THE LANTERNS OF YOUR OWN CORPS.

SO YEAH, I ORDERED THOSE *MURDEROUS GASBAGS OF FEAR* TO BE DROPPED AND DETONATED--AND INSTEAD OF DECIMATING THE ENEMY WE SCARED THE HELL OUTTA THEM AND GOT THEM TO SURRENDER.

A MEANS TO AN END, HMM?

LAST I CHECKED, *ENDING CRAP* WAS PART OF MY JOB DESCRIPTION.

ADIOS, BLUECHACHOS.

CAN I HELP?

WHAT ARE YOU DOING HERE, VANDOR?

I SAW THAT YOU *CANCELLED* LANTERN KIRRT'S HONOR DETAIL.

DIDN'T SEEM RIGHT TO HAVE ANYBODY ELSE GETTING HIS PERSONAL THINGS TOGETHER TO SEND HOME...

WELL, I SEE YOU'VE *FINISHED* BOXING UP MOST OF HIS BELONGINGS.

ACTUALLY, NO, KIRRT WAS SO BUSY PATROLLING HIS SECTOR HE NEVER EVEN GOT AROUND TO *UNPACKING* MOST OF HIS STUFF...

...AND I HAVEN'T BEEN ABLE TO START BECAUSE EVERY TIME I REACH FOR SOMETHING OF HIS, IT HITS ME THAT KIRRT WAS A LANTERN FOR *ONLY* ONE YEAR BECAUSE OF--

STOP BEATING YOURSELF UP. YOU MADE A HARD CHOICE, JOHN--A CHOICE THAT *NEEDED* TO BE MADE.

I *RESPECT* YOU FOR IT.

I'M *NOT* LOOKING FOR RESPECT, VANDOR, I DID WHAT I THOUGHT WAS *RIGHT*...

"...BUT THAT DOESN'T MEAN I HAVE TO LIKE IT."

KRAKK

I THANK *MY* GOD YOU WERE HANGING THERE BESIDE ME WHEN *THE KEEPERS* BROKE KIRRT.

BECAUSE I'M NOT SURE I COULD HAVE DONE WHAT HAD TO BE DONE, AND THEN I WOULD'VE BEEN RESPONSIBLE FOR NOT ONLY THE MURDER OF ALL THOSE PEOPLE THE KEEPERS WERE *DRAINING* TO POWER UP THE STARGATE BUT THE DESTRUCTION OF OA TOO.

I SAY THIS *WITHOUT RESERVATION,* JOHN, THAT IF WE'RE EVER IN THAT SITUATION AGAIN I HOPE YOU'D GIVE ME THE SAME HONOR YOU DID KIRRT BEFORE ALLOWING ME TO BETRAY THE CORPS.

I *DON'T* WANT OR NEED TO BE THE CORPS' CONSCIENCE.

SOMETIMES *SOMEONE* HAS TO BE.

THEN WHY AM I KEEPING WHAT I DID A *SECRET*-- WHY DIDN'T I PUT IT ON MY ACTION REPORT?

ONLY YOU KNOW WHY.

NOW DEPARTING SECTOR 1345 AND CROSSING INTO SECTOR 1346.

SEVEN HOURS UNTIL ARRIVAL AT PLANET LORROR.

FINAL DESTINATION.

APPROACHING THE ORBIT OF PLANET LORROR.

AWAITING DESCENT COMMAND.

STOP RUSHING ME. WE'LL GO DOWN WHEN WE GO DOWN.

ELAPSED TIME IN LORROR'S TROPOSPHERE 32 MINUTES.

WHAT DO YOU WANT ME TO SAY, KIRRT, THAT I'M SORRY?

WELL, I CAN'T DO THAT-- WE BOTH KNOW YOU DIDN'T LEAVE ME ANY OTHER OPTIONS.

WHAT DO YOU SEE, DOGGIES, IS THERE SOME- THING UP--

--HE'S BACK--

MY NAME'S LANTERN STEWART. I'M SO SORRY FOR YOUR LOSS.

...NO... NO...NO...

KIRRT?

WHY'S HE IN THE GREEN GLASS?

HE'S SLEEPING, BIRRT.

WAKE UP, KIRRT--YOU'RE HOME-- WAKE UP.

MISTER LANTERN, HELP HIM GET OUT!

HE CAN'T BREATHE IN THERE--PLEASE, MISTER LANTERN-- DO SOMETHING-- USE YOUR RING!

I CAN'T. YOUR BROTHER'S DEAD, BIRRT. THERE'S NOTHING I CAN DO.

NO HE'S NOT--YOU'RE LYING--

OPEN YOUR EYES, KIRRT!

WAKE UP!

BREAK THE GLASS, KIRRT--FLY OUT!

NIRA!

MA!

LET'S GET HER INSIDE.

MY BOY ALWAYS TRIED TO BE FEARLESS, JUST LIKE ALL OF YOU IN THE CORPS ARE...

PLEASE, DON'T TAKE THIS THE WRONG WAY, SIR, BUT THAT'S A COMMON MISUNDERSTANDING.

WE'RE NOT CHOSEN BECAUSE WE'RE FEARLESS. WE'RE CHOSEN BECAUSE OF OUR ABILITY TO *OVERCOME* GREAT FEAR--TO PUSH PAST IT IN MOMENTS OF LIFE AND DEATH AND TRY TO DO OUR DUTY.

SOMETIMES WE CAN...AND SOMETIMES WE CAN'T.

IF THERE'S ONE THING I'VE LEARNED OVER THE YEARS, IT'S THAT *ONLY* THE DEAD ARE FEARLESS, SIR.

I THINK A SMALL PART OF KIRRT ALWAYS WORRIED HE DIDN'T HAVE WHAT IT TAKES TO BE A LANTERN...

THE MOMENT KIRRT GOT A POWER RING *PROVED* HE HAD WHAT IT TAKES TO BE IN THE CORPS, SIR.

I'M SURE KIRRT WOULD BE HAPPY TO KNOW A VETERAN WHO SPEAKS SO HIGHLY OF HIM IS THE ONE THAT BROUGHT HIM HOME TO US.

I-IT WAS MY HONOR, SIR.

IT'S GOING TO BE HARD ON BIRRT. HE LOOKED UP TO HIS BIG BROTHER. THEY WERE VERY CLOSE. KIRRT WAS ALWAYS THERE FOR HIM... FOR US...

BIRRT, AS YOU MAY HAVE NOTICED, HAS SOME *CHALLENGES* DUE TO BIRTH COMPLICATIONS--KIRRT HELPED HIM FACE THOSE CHALLENGES HEAD ON, BUT NOW...

BIRRT? WHERE ARE YOU?

THE HOVER TRUCK--BIRRT MUST'VE USED IT TO TAKE KIRRT.

DON'T WORRY, SIR. HE CAN'T HAVE GOTTEN FAR.

I'LL HAVE THEM BOTH BACK SOON.

RING, LOCK ON CURRENT POSITION OF LANTERN KIRRT'S COFFIN AND GET ME THERE.

POSITION DETECTED.

LANTERN KIRRT'S COFFIN IS LOCATED BELOW AT THE LORROR QUARRY.

BIRRT, IT'S LANTERN STEWART!

CAN YOU COME OUT SO WE CAN--

GO AWAY!

LEAVE US ALONE!

WHEN A GREEN LANTERN DIES IT GOES OFF INTO SPACE TO FIND A NEW ONE QUICKLY SO THE UNIVERSE CAN ALWAYS BE PROTECTED.

BUT WHY DON'T I HAVE A BROTHER ANYMORE--WHY DID HE HAVE TO DIE, MISTER LANTERN?

KIRRT DIED BECAUSE OF...

BECAUSE WHY?

BECAUSE HE HAD TO BE *REALLY* BRAVE ONE LAST TIME AND BEAT THE BAD GUY...

...SO A LOT OF GOOD PEOPLE COULD LIVE.

SO KIRRT WAS A HERO, RIGHT?

YES.

YES HE WAS.

ARE YOU SURE?

IT'S WHAT HE WOULD'VE WANTED.

ZZRAKK

KIRRT KALLAK
GREEN LANTERN
OF SECTOR 2541

FINISH THE REST, LANTERN STEWART--JUST LIKE WE SAID.

OKAY, BIRRT.

ZZRAKK